THE DReam CHildren

HI, i'm Cleaver and I wanted to tell my story.
As you may not know,I Cleaver Destiny is a no holds bard "Dream Child",now I know your
Wondering,"what oh, what is a Dream Child".?! Well I will tell you,hope your ready to learn-
about the most wonderful thing ever.

A "Dream Child" can enter the kingdom of "TYBELL" by dreaming of "TYBELL"
The magical land where you can think it,then make it true,and the most amazing of all…..
You can bring it back with you.
TYBELL was originally a place for the Diamond fairy tribe.
The last of all the fairy tribes,the most beautiful and powerful and oldest tribe,but no one knows where they went.
My mom told me as a child that she heard that the fairy's imagined they were human but "who knows"?

We also heard the stories about how one evil dream child came back with a kingdom,a horrible fierce army and much riches.
The evil dream child had taken over the whole North,East and west kingdoms of VECKS.
Vecks is my kingdom,well not "my kingdom" but my home,I mean i'm no queen or princess.

BUT I very much love my little land with my parents and my brother reeklo.
All we need are animals and fresh growing crops,maybe new clothes and pots,and pans and…..
There's endless possibilities,I don't see why we couldn't make trees that grow in two days,"no"
maybe one.!

NO,NO,NO! my mom started yelling at me,you cannot use that power Cleaver,! my mom said in,
A mean and upset voice.
That power has a way of taking from your life not giving to it.
Yes you can make things better,but what you give something "has" to take.!
And you might find that you will have to give up too much.
And that power has a way of changing you and not for the better.
Now no more talk of foolishness you silly child,ok mother I replied.

I'm not evil I love everyone why can't my family believe in me ?
Did I do something wrong I wonder?
I can control myself,I'm loving ,I want to help my family and my kingdom.

I'm going to show my family I can help us and bring my own army,a good army and I will save Vecks from the evil dream child. All will see and my family will be happy.
No more scraps of food,"how can you not be happy about food"?
We will all have a celebration,"yeah they will see",my mom I will make queen and my dad king,"yeah they will see".

First I have to meet with my friends and discuss what I should imagine and bring back,everything has to be perfect.
This dream will be much too big to dream up alone,"yeah I got this"!.

Oh, I forgot to tell you,only one dream child is born every thirty years.
The dream child has until death to enter the kingdom of Tybell and imagine.
If you are excepted by evan one past dream child gate keeper when you die, you will remain in TYbell in pure paradise.
And as for your question,can you stay in Tybell while alive?

Why yes of course",but if you stay for even one day it will be one week in the real world.
To stay in Tybell you will leave your love ones.
Nope not for me i need my family and friends.
Oh and when a dream child is born the baby has a glowing birthmark,that glows "sooo "bright that you can't look directly at it.
Don't worry it only glows for the first hour of life,then it is just a birthmark in the shape of the animal that you could shapeshift into,some are born with a person birthmark and can shapeshift from male or female whomever they choose.I was told that you can't bring anyone with you to Tybell,but I wonder has anyone tried?

Time to see my best friend noey she can help me do research to find out or at least help me try on my own.

No maybe i'll ask Dinness he is really good at problem solving and his brother Deek.
Deek is no problem solver or anything he's just the brother,kind of like my brother,just A"
brother".

I'll just call them all, we can figure this out.
And if we do maybe i can take them with me to imagine and maybe with them we can rescue our beloved vecks.

Now later on that day I had planned to meet up with my friends but I accidently fell asleep and entered Tybell.
I never meant to come here now but it was on my mind and now poof"! I'm here.

Oh ,Wow it is sooo beautiful.
All of the beautiful creatures here,what is this?,no what is that?
Everything is so wonderful.

There's so much to see,oh how I wonder what is in that palace that I can see from afar.
I will just go and see for a short second then I will go back.

The palace seems like it keeps getting further and further away ,this is weird i'm going back now!...."wait a minute"! I must have gone back to the wrong place.
Where's my home what is this place?.
""

Mom ,dad ,somebody! Help!

Wait! Am I back? "oh,"NO!
I must have stayed to long!
No,NO,NO!
MOM,DAD! HELP!

This is not a great gift!
This is horrible what do I do now?

I wonder if I can find anyone in my family or any of the family's of my friends I need help from somewhere i'm just a kid.

I see... wait,could that be my brother Reeklo"? He's a very old man but i'd know my brother anywhere.

Reeklo ?
Cleaver?
Yes brother,it is me Cleaver.
What, where have you been?
How could you leave us? your disappearence destroyed ma ma, and dad went looking for you.
He never returned.

What happened to this place reeko?

The evil dream child has taken over the entire world past vecks,well what use to be vecks.

The evil dream child found a way to take the life force from the newest dream child and made himself young again.you must hide and tell no one of who you are .the evil dream child will surely come after you.

Now if you want to know what happens next wait for part 2 THE ALPHA CHILD

www.ingramcontent.com/pod-product-compliance
Lightning Source LLC
Chambersburg PA
CBHW040037240726
48664CB00003B/961